Judith Harries

Series editor
ALISTAIR
BRYCE-CLEGG

fantastic ideas for
making music

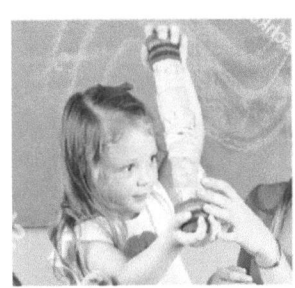
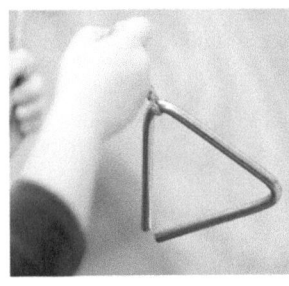

FEATHERSTONE

FEATHERSTONE
Bloomsbury Publishing Plc
50 Bedford Square, London, WC1B 3DP, UK
29 Earlsfort Terrace, Dublin 2, Ireland

BLOOMSBURY, FEATHERSTONE and the Feather logo are trademarks of Bloomsbury Publishing Plc

First published in Great Britain, 2021 by Bloomsbury Publishing Plc

A catalogue record for this book is available from the British Library

ISBN: PB: 978-1-4729-8411-1; ePDF: 978-1-4729-8409-8

2 4 6 8 10 9 7 5 3 1

Designed by Lynda Murray
Printed and bound in India by Replika Press Pvt. Ltd.

To find out more about our authors and books visit www.bloomsbury.com and sign up for
our newsletters

Contents

Introduction

Music is an essential part of human life. Extensive research has shown the comprehensive benefits of music: it affects our mood, moves us to dance and sing; increases brain power and learning potential, and involves us in social activity that feels uplifting. Joint music-making promotes cooperative behaviour in all ages.

Children 'do' or experience music in different ways every day. The term 'musicking' was coined by musician and educator Christopher Small to describe children's engagement with music as they play, sing, dance, listen to and compose music (*Musicking*, 1998). The activities in this book seek to engage children in a wealth of musical experiences that will set them on their own musical journey.

Early Years Foundation Stage (EYFS) settings are currently challenged to provide continuous provision for many areas of the curriculum, and music can be included in this. Self-initiated musical play can be integrated into everyday ongoing activities. Look at some helpful ideas for continuous provision in 'Sound effects station' (page 50) and 'Just jamming' (page 57). Take care to provide good quality instruments and add new musical sounds each week for children to explore. Take an interest in children's interactions with musical instruments, be prepared to play yourself, and join in as a musical partner. This will help children to see that you value their musical contributions.

The activities in this collection are organised into sections to guide you, from practising vocal sounds and singing, through to learning about rhythm and using instruments to make music together. The activities in the 'Conducting counts' and 'Mixing media' sections feature ideas on how to organise musical sounds as the children learn to play together. There are also lots of opportunities to make

instruments outlined in 'Maraca madness' (page 27), 'Great guiros' (page 9), 'Music workshop' (page 42) and 'Design your own instrument' (page 45).

Making music together and performing to others is essential as it helps children experience what it's like to be a musician. Lots of activities in the book encourage this: 'Leader of the band' (page 40), 'Time to play together' (page 60) and the activities in the 'Around the world' section. The book can be dipped into as a collection of resources or worked through in a more progressive way.

In *Musical Development Matters in the Early Years*, Nicola Burke recognises that 'music interweaves through all areas of learning and development'. Enjoy using these 50 fantastic musical activities with the children in your setting to enrich their lives and experiences.

Small, C. (1998). *Musicking: The Meanings of Performing and Listening*. Wesleyan University Press.

Burke, N. (2018). *Musical Development Matters in the Early Years*. The British Association for Early Childhood Education.

Musical terms

Here are some simple definitions of musical terms used in the book:

- **Pulse:** a steady beat in music, like a heartbeat
- **Rhythm:** patterns of short and long sounds
- **Pitch**: how high or low a note sounds
- **Dynamics:** how loudly or quietly music is played
- **Tempo:** the speed of the music
- **Timbre:** the quality of the sound, e.g. the difference between the same note being played on different instruments
- **Structure:** how to organise sounds, sometimes shown with letters like ABA
- **Genre:** the style of music, e.g. pop, classical, jazz, folk
- **Pentatonic scale:** a sequence of five musical notes in an octave

Useful resources

Most resources will be easily accessible and may already be available in your setting. It is, however, important to have a selection of good-quality musical instruments.

- **Untuned:** maracas, natural shakers, claves, wood blocks, cowbells, tambourines, guiros, cabasas, castanets, triangles, agogô bells, jingle bells, hand cymbals, hand drums, coconuts, a large gathering drum.
- **Tuned:** xylophones, glockenspiels, chime bars, hand chimes, kalimbas (a type of thumb piano), Boomwhackers®.

Remember to collect recycled materials to use when making DIY instruments. For example: plastic bottles, lids, containers, boxes, tins, elastic bands, textured papers and shaker fillings (rice, lentils, etc.).

How to use this book

It is a good idea to read through each activity before you start in case you want to change the order or just focus on one part. Anything is possible! The pages are all organized in the same way.

What you need lists the resources needed for each activity. These are likely to be readily available in most settings or can be bought or made easily. See the suggestions on this page for ideas.

What to do provides step-by-step instructions. It often includes references to well-known songs or new songs, written especially for this book. Some of these use the tunes of traditional songs, others can be chanted in rhythm or sung to a tune of your own making.

Taking it forward does exactly that – takes the activity to another level, often by introducing ideas for songs, performances and stories to enrich the children's experience or suggesting further activities related to the original idea.

What's in it for the children? lists some of the benefits the children will gain through the activities and how they will contribute to their learning. These are useful to share with other staff and parents.

Top tip gives a brief word of advice or helpful tip that could make all the difference to the experience of the activity for you and the children.

Health & Safety is only included if there are particular issues to be noted and addressed above and beyond usual health and safety measures.

Warming up
Getting ready to sing

What you need:

- A puppet with a moving mouth (a 'singing puppet')
- Card and felt-tip pens

Top tip

Always start with a physical warm-up before warming up the voice. Try wiggling and shaking each part of the body from the toes all the way up to the head!

Health & Safety

Make sure children don't force their voices. Always have water available to drink during singing sessions.

What to do:

1. Invite the children to stand in a circle so everybody can see each other. Introduce the children to the singing puppet. Can the children give it a name? Use the singing puppet to model the warm-up activities. You could record examples of the warm-up activities so children can listen and sing along.

2. Start with the game 'Grins and grimaces' to warm up the face and mouth muscles. Ask the children to make the biggest grin possible, like a Halloween pumpkin. Follow that by making a grimace by screwing up the face as small as possible. Repeat.

3. Try some 'bubble singing'. Start with lip trills made by vibrating the lips together. If the children find this tricky, they can try pushing up both their cheeks with two fingers.

4. Invite the children to sing different notes through the lip trills. It should feel and sound 'bubbly'! Can they copy a sequence of notes, stepping from low to high or jumping from high to low?

5. Move onto 'sirens sing'. Ask the children to say the word 'sing' and stay on the 'ng' sound to create a siren sound. Change the pitch of the siren sound from high to low, using hand gestures to show the sound changing.

6. Invite the children to pretend that their index finger is a whiteboard pen. Can they write their name or initials in the air using their pen and the siren voice?

What's in it for the children?

This activity develops vocal skills and teaches children that it is vital to warm up the voice before singing.

Taking it forward

- Draw arrows, hills, valleys and steps on card for the children to follow as they sing. Can they make their voices go on a journey – up and down in pitch – as you follow the pitch line with your finger? Invite the children to draw and sing their own pitch lines or journeys.

- Sing the following song to the tune of 'I Can Sing a Rainbow':

  Sing some sounds and bubbles too

  High and low, fast and slow, sing!

  I can sing a siren, sing a siren, sing a siren too.

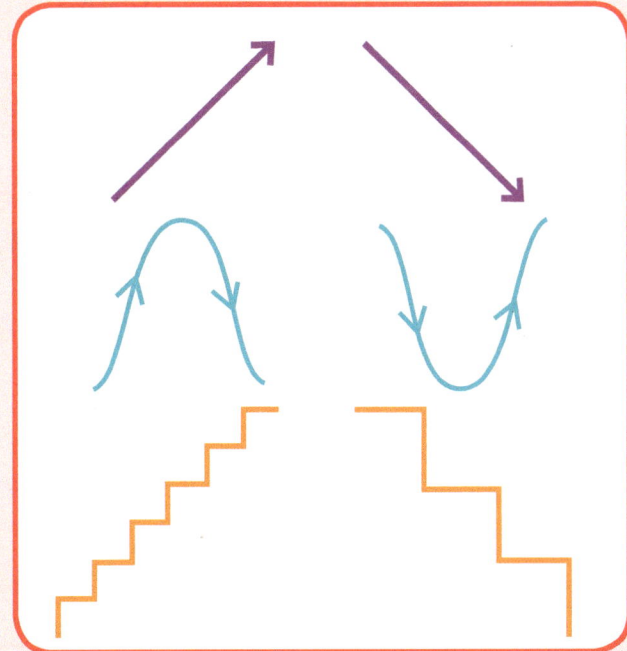

Nursery rhymes and songs

Singing well-known songs together

What you need:

- A selection of nursery rhymes, available on the BBC Teach 'School Radio' website and online.
- Nursery rhyme posters, pictures and books
- A singing puppet
- A carpet tile to use for a performance mat
- A recording device (e.g. a tablet)
- A plastic microphone

Top tip

When singing songs and rhymes all together, use one phrase that signals the start such as 'off we go'.

What's in it for the children?

Children will be able to recite and sing a wide selection of nursery rhymes and songs.

Taking it forward

- Provide a carpet tile as a performance 'song mat' for the children to stand on and sing their rhymes or songs to the group. Record them performing (see 'The recording studio', page 46).
- Make a class book of the children's favourite songs. Invite the children to draw illustrations and add photos of them singing. Use the songbook to help them choose songs to sing every day.

What to do:

1. Share some well-known nursery rhymes with the children, such as 'Baa Baa Black Sheep', 'Humpty Dumpty', 'Twinkle Twinkle Little Star' and 'Hey Diddle Diddle'. Repeat the songs over and over again to help the children learn the words and the tune.

2. Provide posters and books of nursery rhymes and songs for the children to share.

3. Try some counting songs: '1, 2, 3, 4, 5', 'Ten Fat Sausages', 'Five Little Peas', 'Five Little Ducks', 'Five Little Men in a Flying Saucer', 'Hickory Dickory Dock' and so on.

4. Sing and move to body songs: 'Heads, Shoulders, Knees and Toes', 'Ten Little Fingers', 'One Finger, One Thumb', 'If You're Happy and You Know It', etc.

5. Have fun with animal songs: 'Old MacDonald', 'The Animal Fair', 'One Grey Elephant Balancing', 'Five Little Monkeys' and many more.

6. Let the singing puppet and the children choose their favourite nursery rhymes and well-known songs. Invite them to sing the following song to the tune of 'When the Saints Go Marching In':

    I like to sing,

    I like to sing,

    I like to sing a song with you,

    And my favourite song to sing is…

7. Display the results on a bar chart of 'My Favourite Song'.

Singing games

Playing games with a song attached

What you need:

- A long loop of string or stretchy elastic with a large button or cotton reel threaded onto it
- A plate or bowl

Top tip

Always teach the song first and when the children are more confident, play the game.

What's in it for the children?

These games teach children how to take turns, listen, use their imagination and keep a beat.

Taking it forward

- Work with the children to make up a new singing game. Choose something to pass around the circle, openly or hidden, as a basis for the game. Choose a familiar tune and make up some new words (see 'Write your own songs', page 10).

- Try a listening game of 'Odd one out'. Sing three sounds, two the same and one different. Can the children identify the odd one out?

What to do:

1. Learn the song 'Pass the Button Round' to the tune of 'Wind the Bobbin Up':

   Pass the button round,
   Pass the button round,
   Pull, pull, hold it tight!

2. Ask the children to sit in a circle and hold onto a loop of string or stretchy elastic with a button threaded onto it. Practise moving the button along the string and sing the song.

3. Invite a child to sit in the middle and cover their eyes. The rest of the children sing the song, moving the button along. The child holding the button on the word 'tight' hides the button in their fist. Can the child in the middle guess who has the button? The child who had the button sits in the middle for the next round.

4. Learn the song 'How I'd Love some Apple Pie' to the tune of 'Rain, Rain, Go Away'. Pass an empty plate or bowl around the circle in time to the beat of the song:

   Oh me, oh my,
   How I'd love some apple pie

5. Let the children take turns to replace the word 'apple' with a different food.

6. Learn the song 'Time to Pack a Picnic' and chant it in rhythm:

   Time to pack a picnic, don't be slow.
   The sun is shining so off we go.
   Don't forget the sandwiches
   Yes, I've packed the sandwiches

   Can the children replace 'sandwiches' with different food?

7. Repeat the last two lines over and over as you accumulate a number of picnic items.

Write your own songs

Adding new words to existing tunes

Top tip ⭐

Use tunes that you and the children already know; nursery rhymes; traditional songs and even pop songs all work well. Search online if you need help remembering the tunes.

What's in it for the children?

Singing songs together definitely makes routines seem more fun and it also helps children learn how to follow instructions. Adding their own words to tunes will help children develop communication and language skills.

Taking it forward

- Provide the children with some pitched instruments such as a xylophone or keyboard. (see 'Playing with pitch', page 34). Encourage them to make up some new tunes as well.

- Try some call and response songs where the children respond with a repeated phrase to everything the 'caller' sings. For example, when the caller sings 'Tidy up the bricks, please' or 'Tidy up the home corner', the children respond with 'Time to tidy up'.

What to do:

1. Start with a 'Singing register' to welcome the children at the start of each session. Sing the song to the tune of 'Pop Goes the Weasel', adding the children's names and personalising the last line:

   Hello, hello [child's name] x3

   Welcome to [day of the week, name of class or school, etc.]

2. Think of some other routines that could be made more fun by adding a song: lining up, home time, sitting on the carpet, and so on.

3. Create songs for topics that you are exploring in your setting by choosing a familiar tune and adding new words. Keep it simple.

4. Involve the children in the choice of tunes and the writing of new lyrics. Get the singing puppet to join in.

Hear me hum

Copying some humming and singing sounds

What you need:

- A singing puppet

Top tip

Take time to practise operating the singing puppet in front of a mirror at home if you are not very confident.

What's in it for the children?

Children will use their singing voices to practise pitch-matching and echoing simple patterns.

Taking it forward

- Invite the children to take turns leading the echo singing and sing a two-note pattern for the group to echo.

- Sing some echo songs such as 'Charlie Over the Ocean' or 'Sing After Me' with Ernie and Elmo from *Sesame Street*. You could listen to some music inspired by the cuckoo call such as 'The Cuckoo' from 'The Carnival of the Animals' by Saint-Saëns. You could also listen to the song 'Do-Re-Mi' from *The Sound of Music* by Rodgers and Hammerstein.

- Help the children to make their own singing puppet using old socks, buttons for eyes and noses, and felt ears. Can they make their puppets sing?

What to do:

1. Show the children how to hum by making an 'mm' sound through closed lips. Ask them to copy you and echo humming and buzzing sounds.

2. Use the singing puppet to model echoing vocal sounds. Make the puppet hum something and then show the children how to echo it perfectly.

3. Try some echo singing using two notes, G and E, easily recognised as the 'cuckoo call'. Try singing the notes using two nonsense syllables such as 'dee' and 'dum'. Try it in a scat or improvised singing style.

4. Replace the nonsense syllables with the words 'so' and 'mi' to represent the notes G and E. This introduces the children to the Solfège method (Do, Re, Mi, Fa, So, La, Ti).

5. Add hand signs:
   - 'So': Place your hand flat and on its side with your fingers stacked, your thumb at the top and little finger at the bottom.
   - 'Mi': Place your hand flat out in front of you, palm facing down.

6. Invite the children to work with a 'singing partner'. One child sings a pattern using 'so' and 'mi' sounds, which their partner echoes.

Improvising vocal sounds

Experimenting freely with voices

What you need:

- A singing puppet
- Handheld mirrors
- A plastic microphone
- A recording device (e.g. a tablet)

Top tip ⭐

If some children are hesitant or shy to experiment with their voices, suggest they try with their eyes closed.

What's in it for the children?

Children will feel confident enough to discover new ways to use their voices and create vocal sounds.

Taking it forward

- Record the children speaking and making sounds. Play them back. Do they recognise themselves or each other?

- Try a game of 'Good afternoon, your majesty'. Choose one child to be king or queen. They face the wall while another child speaks using a silly voice as a disguise. Can the king or queen recognise who is speaking?

- Search online for 'Voices Around the World' and listen to the variety of voices with the children.

What to do:

1. Sitting on the floor in a circle, invite the children to copy some different vocal sounds, such as sirens, doorbells, machines, creaking doors, owl hoots, other animal sounds, etc.

2. Start a game of 'Pass a sound around'. Try passing a 'moo', 'growl' or 'meow' around the circle.

3. Repeat using sound words such as 'pop', 'hiss', and 'bang' or make phonic sounds with your voice for the children to copy. Try long vowel sounds – 'oo', 'ah', 'ee' – or short consonant sounds such as 't', 'p' and 'k'.

4. Sing the song 'Make Some Noise':

   Make some noise

   With your voice

   Loud or quiet

   It's your choice!

   Chant the song and replace 'loud or quiet' with alternatives such as 'high or low', 'happy or sad' and 'long or short'.

5. Can the children invent their own vocal sounds to show the group? Model using the singing puppet. Encourage the children to experiment and allow time for improvisation!

6. Provide handheld mirrors so the children can watch their mouths as they make each different sound.

7. Pass a plastic microphone around the circle so the children can make a louder sound.

Vocal beatboxing

Using singing voices like vocal percussion

What you need:

- **Examples of beatboxing (available online)**
- **A singing puppet**
- **Cardboard circles**

Top tip

Don't worry if you think you can't sing: children will love your voice. Enjoy experimenting with vocal sounds yourself.

What's in it for the children?

Children can explore different ways of using their voice to make rhythmic sound effects. This may also help improve children's articulation and clarity of speaking voice.

Taking it forward

- Play 'Musical beatbox'. Write the beatbox sounds ('bu', 'k' and 'ts') onto large cardboard circles. Place them on the floor randomly. Play some music and invite the children to dance until the music stops and then land on the nearest circle and carry on the music making their beatbox sound.

- Experiment by adding other beatbox sounds such as 'pf' and 'ch'.

What to do:

1. Start with a warm-up song to explore using voices in different ways:

   (Adult) *Can you use your talking voice, just like me?*

   (Children) *I can use my talking voice, you will see.*

   Replace 'talking voice' with alternatives such as 'whispering voice', 'angry voice' or 'squeaky voice'.

2. Listen to some examples of beatboxing.

3. Say some simple words: boots and cats. Ask the children to echo you. Say each word four times. Now try to emphasise the initial consonant so it sounds more like 'bu' and 'k'. Model the sounds using the singing puppet.

4. Make up rhythm patterns using the words 'boots, cats, boots, cats' and try saying them together as a group.

5. Now emphasise the end of the words – 'ts' – and practise the sounds.

6. Ask the children to copy some other simple patterns of beatbox sounds, such as 'bu bu k' and 'k ts k ts' . Experiment by making the consonant sounds bigger or louder. Can the children make them sound more like a drum or a cymbal?

7. Invite the children to invent their own beatbox patterns for the group to copy.

Keeping the beat

Feeling and marking the beat with actions

What you need:

- Music with a strong beat
- Red paper or cardboard
- A heart template
- Scissors
- Bean bags or soft toys

Top tip

Try sitting in a circle listening to music with a strong beat and observe the children's physical responses: tapping feet, nodding heads, and so on.

What to do:

1. Sit in a circle and listen to some music with a strong beat. This could be classical or pop music, such as 'March' from *The Nutcracker* by Tchaikovsky or 'Happy' by Pharrell Williams.

2. Invite the children to tap their knees like drums in time to the beat or pulse of the music.

3. Move on to tap other parts of the body and ask children to copy – heads, shoulders, elbows, tummy, feet, and so on.

4. Sing the following song to the tune of 'If You're Happy and You Know It', changing the actions to use different body parts:

   If you can feel the beat, clap your hands, (x2)

   If you can feel the beat, clap your hands and tap your feet.

   If you can feel the beat, clap your hands.

5. Help the children to cut out heart shapes from red paper or cardboard. Show them how to make the hearts 'pulse' or move in time to the beat of the music by moving them up and down, or in and out.

6. Provide bean bags or soft toys. Choose a different part of the body to tap with the bean bag – hands, heads, knees, and so on.

7. Play 'Follow the beat-leader'. Invite the children to take turns leading and choosing which body part to tap for the rest of the group to copy.

Health & Safety

Take care using scissors. Provide left-handed scissors where required.

What's in it for the children?

Children will be able to develop their understanding of the beat or pulse in music and respond to it with large and small movements.

Taking it forward

- Try moving in different ways to the beat. March on the spot, move like soldiers, stretch the arms up high, mime using brooms to sweep, jump up and down, hop on one leg, and so on.

- Sing some train songs as the children move around to the beat. Try 'Get on Board, Little Children' or 'Train is A Comin''.

- Extend the 'Follow the beat-leader' game by asking the leader to choose an action as they lead the children around the room.

Body percussion

Exploring different body beats using hands and feet

What you need:

- A recording device (e.g. a tablet)
- A large sheet of paper
- Paints
- Felt-tip pens

Top tip

Try out some sounds yourself using your hands, feet, and body, before asking the children for their ideas, so you are prepared for any surprise sounds!

What's in it for the children?

This will develop physical coordination and at the same time encourage children to use their imagination to create new sounds.

Taking it forward

- Create a 'body beats orchestra'. Divide the children into three groups and give each group a different hand or foot sound to make in time to the beat. For example, group one claps their hands in time to the beat (1, 2, 3, 4), group two stamps their feet on '1' and group three rubs their hands together on '2' and '4'. Swap!

- Make a body percussion map. Ask a volunteer to lie down on a piece of paper and invite the children to draw around their body shape. Paint the shape and label all the body percussion sounds the children have discovered.

- Show the children the body percussion piece 'Connect It' by Anna Meredith, available online.

What to do:

1. Ask the children to explore how many different sounds they can make using their hands. Try clapping, tapping with two fingers against a palm, finger clicking, patting or slapping different parts of body, rubbing hands together, knocking fists together, and so on.

2. Go around the circle and invite the children to demonstrate a hand sound to the group. Sing the song 'Make a Sound' to the tune of 'I Hear Thunder':

   Make a sound (x2)
   With your hands (x2)
   I can make this sound: [demo sound]
   You can too, me and you.

3. Invite the children to repeat the song with different body parts. They could use their feet (stamping or rubbing), mouths (clicking or tapping their mouths) or their bodies (patting their arms or knees).

4. Invite the children to work with a partner and create a simple pattern using two contrasting body percussion sounds.

5. Record the partner work on a tablet and listen back to it as a group.

Stamp, clap, click, tap

Creating a body beat groove

What you need:

- Strips of paper or card
- Felt-tip pens
- A drum (or a song with a strong beat)
- A recording device (e.g. a tablet)

Top tip ⭐

If children find it difficult to click their fingers, suggest that they mime the action or click their tongue instead.

What's in it for the children?

Children will be able to invent and repeat a pattern of sounds in time to the beat. They will learn how to take turns and work together as a large group.

Taking it forward

- Challenge the children to create ways to notate the body percussion patterns. Can they draw or notate a pattern onto a strip of paper divided into four parts for others to copy? See 'Notation notes', page 49.
- Show examples of body percussion in music, such as 'Clapping Music' by Steve Reich or Pentatonix's cover of 'White Winter Hymnal' by Fleet Foxes, available online.

What to do:

1. Ask the children to stand in a circle. Try some 'echo clapping' by inviting them to copy a simple pattern that you make, for example, four claps or four stamps.

2. Try a 'Mexican clap wave'. Ask each child to take it in turn to clap once and pass the clap around the circle. Repeat with a stamp. Can they do it in time to the beat of a drum?

3. Working with a partner, let the children choose a pattern using two sounds to send around the circle, for instance 'clap, tap'.

4. Create a 'body beat groove' by showing the children a pattern of body percussion sounds: stamp, clap, click, tap. Practise repeating the pattern.

5. Ask the children to make up their own body beat groove patterns using four different sounds. Can they teach it to the group? Try repeating it in time to a drum or a song with a strong beat.

6. Sing a song to go alongside the activity, replacing the lines in bold with whatever patterns the children have created:

   We can make a body beat
   Pass it round the ring
   This is our new body beat
   Listen as we sing.
   Stamp, clap, click, tap
   Pass it round the ring.
   Stamp, clap, click, tap
   Listen as we sing.

7. Record some of the body beat grooves and listen back.

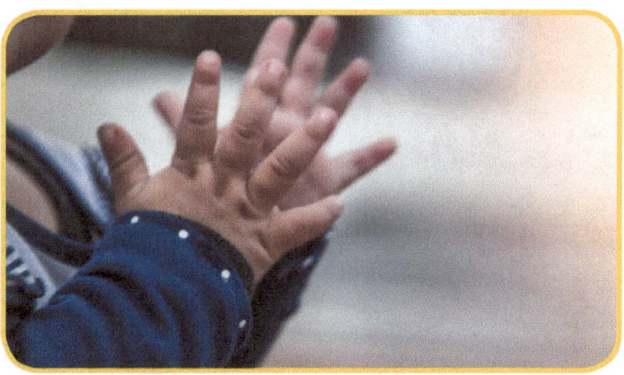

Repeat after me

Developing listening and echo clapping skills

What you need:

- Lots of simple rhythms to clap

Top tip

Use a quick shorthand to notate some rhythms to clap before you start. Use lines to represent long sounds and dots to represent short sounds. For example, '_ _ . .' (long, long, short, short).

What to do:

1. Practise some echo clapping (see 'Stamp, clap, click, tap', page 17). Use the phrase 'Repeat after me' to show that the game is about to begin.

2. Start by clapping a steady four claps on the beat for the children to copy. Signal for the children to echo you by opening both your palms.

3. Try some simple rhythm patterns using long and short sounds (see the 'Top tip'). Vary the rhythms by thinking of words with different numbers of syllables. For example, 'pepperoni pizza': '.... _ _'.

4. Show children how to tap two fingers into the palm of their hand to introduce quiet tapping sounds to the echo patterns.

5. Mix it up with loud claps and quiet taps. Talk to the children about dynamics (see 'Musical terms', page 5).

6. Invite the children to take turns leading the echo clapping and tapping.

7. Chant a song to accompany the clapping:
   Repeat after me: 1, 2, 3, 4
   Try it again: 1, 2 and 3, 4
   Turn it around: 1, 2, 3 and 4
   Copy the sound: 1 and 2 and 3 and 4.

What's in it for the children?

Children will be able to listen carefully to simple rhythms and clap them back accurately.

Taking it forward

- Play 'Stop, don't, clap that one'. Say and clap this phrase over and over (_ _ .. _). Clap a series of different patterns for children to clap back to you. They should copy all the patterns except the one that you practised at the beginning. When they hear this pattern invite them to chant the words 'Stop, don't, clap that one' back to you instead of clapping. Can you catch them out?

- Play the game again, this time choosing a different rhythm not to echo and call it the 'forbidden rhythm'.

- Listen to music that uses repetition, such as 'Around the World' by Daft Punk.

All in the name

Exploring rhythm with words

Top tip

Introduce word rhythms to fit in with topics, for example food: 'I like fish and chips'; transport: 'Waiting at the station'; weather: 'Look out for rainbows', and so on.

What's in it for the children?

Children will learn to recognise that words have rhythms and use them to create rhythm patterns.

Taking it forward

- Invite the children to read and clap the word rhythm of a friend's name.

- Play 'Broken phone'. Whisper a word rhythm to the child next to you and ask them to whisper it to their neighbour. Can it pass all the way around the circle without changing? Try passing a tapped rhythm around the circle.

- Listen to some rhythmic Latin American music such as samba. Also check out 'Samba Samba' by The Gipsy Kings and 'I Got Rhythm' by George Gershwin.

What to do:

1. Invite the children to sit in a circle. Place all the children's name cards in the middle and ask them to take turns to find their own name.

2. Show the children how to clap the rhythm of their name by clapping the syllables.

3. Start a repeated pattern of two claps and then count to two in the pause before the next two claps. Ask the children to take turns to clap their name in the pause.

4. Pass a drum or tambourine around the circle and chant the song 'All in the Name':

   Play the game, what's your name?

   Can you hear the rhythm?

   Play the drum, [child's name]

   It's all in the name.

   When you get to the line 'Play the drum', invite the child holding the instrument to tap their name on the drum. For example, one tap for the name 'Max' and three taps for 'Samina'.

5. Use some other word phrases to practise clapping word rhythms. Try 'I like clapping games', 'Can you hear the beat?' or 'Singing songs is good for you'.

6. Try clapping in two groups. One group claps a pattern four times and the other group claps a different pattern four times. Can both groups clap their patterns at the same time?

7. Play 'Clap in the gap'. Start a repeated pattern of four claps and then count to four to create a gap before the next four claps. Ask the children to take turns to clap a rhythm in the gap. Remind them that if they cannot think of a rhythm, they can clap four times and it will fit!

Ostinato loops
Clapping repeated patterns

What you need:

- Recording software, such as Audacity® or GarageBand® (optional)
- A tablet (optional)

Top tip

An ostinato (meaning 'obstinate') is a pattern that is played over and over.

What's in it for the children?

Children will be able to recognise and perform a repeated clapping pattern and keep it going.

Taking it forward

- Working with a partner, invite the children to play clapping games such as 'A Sailor Went to Sea'. Show them the video 'Epic Patty Cake Song (I'll Think Of You)' by Kurt Hugo Schneider on YouTube.

- Record the children's clapping patterns and turn them into loops using recording software such as Audacity® or GarageBand®.

- Let the children use apps such as Loopimal™, Toc and Roll™ or Jelly Band™ to create ostinatos and loops (see 'The recording studio', page 46).

What to do:

1. Sit the children in a circle and try some echo clapping (see 'Stamp, clap, click, tap', page 17).

2. Clap one rhythm pattern over and over again. Ask the children if they notice anything different.

3. Explain that when one pattern is repeated over and over again, it is called an ostinato, loop or riff.

4. Play 'Sticky loops'. Clap some patterns and invite the children to clap them back, listening out for repetition. When you clap the same pattern three times or more, you are stuck in a 'sticky loop', and the children can show you they have noticed by putting their hands on their heads and not copying any longer.

5. Divide the children into two groups and use an ostinato or repeated pattern to accompany a song. Ask one group to clap 'tick tock tick tock' while another group sings the song 'Hickory Dickory Dock'.

6. Ask the other group to chant 'marching, marching' while the other sings 'The Grand Old Duke of York'.

7. Sing the following song to the tune of 'Twinkle Twinkle Little Star':
   Can you clap this after me?
   (Clap a pattern)
   Clap it again and you will see:
   (Repeat the pattern)
   You have made a loop of three:
   (Repeat the pattern)

Time for action

Moving to some action songs

What you need:

- A selection of action and circle songs
- A singing puppet
- Live or recorded music

Top tip

Circle songs and games are a good way to begin or end a music session, helping everybody to work together.

What to do:

1. Ask the children to stand in a circle and warm up their bodies and voices using some ideas from 'Warming up', page 6.

2. Start with a movement version of 'Simon says'. You could start with 'Simon says shrug your shoulders'. Involve the singing puppet in leading the game, using the puppet's name instead of Simon.

3. Try a musical version of the game, using 'Mrs Music' or 'Mr Music'. For example, 'Mrs Music says make some noise with your feet'.

4. Try some action songs involving the body such as 'Heads, Shoulders, Knees and Toes' or 'Peter Hammers'.

5. Sing some animal songs such as 'Sleeping Bunnies' or 'Five Little Speckled Frogs'.

6. Move onto circle songs with actions such as 'The Hokey Cokey', 'Here We Go Looby Loo', 'The Farmer's in His Den' and 'Here We Go Round the Mulberry Bush'.

7. Try some traditional circle dances such as 'In and Out the Dusty Bluebells' and 'Ring a Ring o' Roses'.

8. Choose a song known to the children and add new actions. Try to use their ideas wherever possible.

What's in it for the children?

Children will be encouraged to use their bodies to add actions to songs and games, promoting physical activity and memory.

Taking it forward

- Let the children have fun doing opposite actions to a song. Swap ups for downs and even arms for legs!

- Try writing a brand-new action song using a well-known tune. See 'Write your own songs', page 10.

- Try some parachute games, moving the parachute up and down in time to the beat of the music.

- Find a selection of action songs on the BBC Teach channel on YouTube.

Dancing shoes

Trying some simple dance moves

What you need:

- Space to dance
- Lots of different dance music
- Props (wrist or ankle bells, scarves, hula hoops and ribbons)

Top tip

Relate dance activities to the different topics in your setting. Some children may go to dance classes, such as ballet or street. Let them share their skills with other children.

What to do:

1. Warm up using ideas from 'Music on the move', page 26.

2. Ask the children to find a partner and stand facing each other. Choose one child to be the 'dancer' and challenge their partner to copy all their moves like a mirror.

3. Invent a sequence of moves for the children to copy with their partner. Try four claps, four jumps, two spins and four steps on the spot.

4. Invite the children to choose some dance music to use from a selection of songs. Ask them to create their own sequence using their own ideas.

5. Let the children use different props to add to their dance moves. For example, provide each pair of children with a hula hoop. Ask them to hold onto the hoop, standing opposite each other, and slowly move it through their fingers as they walk or dance around in a circle.

6. Stand in a circle. Give each child a scarf or a ribbon and invite them to wave the scarves up and down, in and out of the circle, spin round and sit down. Can they pretend the ribbon is a tail wiggling behind them? Invite the children to run around and try twisting, twirling, skipping, and leaping.

✚ Health & Safety

Remind children to take care as they move around, particularly when they are using props.

What's in it for the children?

Children will be able to move in time to music and create simple dance moves together.

Taking it forward

- Play some games to reinforce the children's knowledge of left and right. Show them how to hold up their left-hand thumb and index finger to make an 'L'. Tie a ribbon on each child's left wrist or give them bells to wear on their left wrist.

- Help the children to understand clockwise and anticlockwise movements by standing in a circle and all moving together clockwise, then anticlockwise.

- Watch different dances from around the world online, such as flamenco, samba, Bollywood or morris dancing.

Music on the move

Simple music and movement starters

What you need:

- A tambourine
- A guiro
- Handheld instruments such as claves and shakers
- Recorded music: music with a strong beat and with different tempos

What's in it for the children?

Children will be able to move in different ways, safely negotiating space and responding to music with different beats, tempos and timbres.

Taking it forward

- Provide the children with handheld instruments such as shakers (see 'Maraca madness', page 27) or claves. Make some music on the move.
- Invite the children to choose movements to match different styles of music. How do they want to move to different pieces?

Health & Safety

Remind children to take care as they move around each other, particularly when they are holding musical instruments.

What to do:

1. Invite all the children to find a space to stand on their own. Ask them to stretch out their arms and check that they cannot touch anybody else.

2. Start with a simple warm-up. Shake a tambourine and ask the children to wiggle all the different parts of their bodies. Can they freeze every time the tambourine stops?

3. Try some shoulder boogies. Sing the following song to the tune of 'London Bridge is Falling Down' and play the guiro to accompany it:

   Shrug your shoulders up and down,

   Up and down, up and down.

   Shrug your shoulders up and down,

   Do the shoulder boogie.

4. Walk on the spot and play some music with a strong beat to establish a pulse. Add swinging arms and turn it into a marching move. Speed up and walk twice as fast to the same beat.

5. Challenge the children to move around the room in different ways: jogging, skipping, crawling, sliding on their backs, creeping on their tiptoes, etc. Change the movement and tempo to match different styles of music.

Maraca madness

Making a collection of shakers

What you need:

- Maracas: plastic, wooden or homemade
- A selection of empty containers, bottles, cardboard containers with metal bottoms, etc.
- Fillings: dry rice, beans, lentils, pebbles, sand, gravel, beads, etc.
- Resources to make natural shakers (optional)

What's in it for the children?

Children will improve their coordination and develop both large and small movements by playing maracas and making their own shakers.

Taking it forward

- Play 'Shaker pairs'. Fill identical plastic containers with pairs of distinctive sounds, such as dry rice, coins, or sand. Can the children find pairs of matching shakers just by listening to the timbre (see Musical Terms, page 5)?

- Make a natural shaker by growing (or buying) a gourd. Cut a small hole in the base, scoop out the pulp and leave it to dry. Fill it with a handful of gravel, tape up the hole and cover the gourd with a coat of varnish.

- Listen to some salsa music which features the maraca.

What to do:

1. Ask the children to sit in a circle and place a maraca or shaker in front of each child.

2. Invite all the children to pick up the maracas and shake them all together. Refer to 'Start and stop', page 38, for some useful hand signals to conduct musical sounds.

3. Play 'I've got a shaker!'. Ask each child to take turns to shake their maraca one at a time. Can they hear the different sounds each maraca makes?

4. Sing the song 'I've Got a Shaker' to the tune of 'When the Saints Go Marching In':

   I've got a shaker, (x2)

   I've got a shaker in my hand,

   Can you hear the shaking maracas

   As we shake them all around?

5. Try some echo shaking. Shake a pattern on the maraca and invite the children to echo it. Try different ways of playing the maracas, such as shaking them gently or tapping them onto your other hand.

6. Open a maraca madness workshop with lots of different containers and fillings for the children to make their own DIY shakers.

Shake, rattle 'n' roll

Making upcycled instruments together

What you need:

- A selection of musical instruments to shake
- Small bottles, bowls or jugs
- Large, clear plastic bottles or cardboard tubes
- A variety of natural fillings: rice, beans, pasta, lentils, pebbles, gravel, conkers, pinecones, feathers, sand, etc.
- A variety of other materials: beads, bottle tops, buttons, sequins, silver foil, coins, screws and bolts
- Glue or sticky tape

What to do:

1. Let the children experiment by shaking a selection of musical instruments, such as maracas, bells, tambourines, shekere, rain sticks, nut or seed shakers, etc. Which rattling sounds do they prefer?

2. Explain to the children that they are going to make their own 'shaker-rattle 'n' roller'. Play different versions of the song 'Shake, Rattle and Roll' by Big Joe Turner, Bill Haley and Elvis Presley to the children.

3. Set up a sound station with trays of different materials for the children to explore. Show them how to pour a few items into a small bottle, bowl or jug and shake to hear the different sounds they can create.

4. Invite them to choose their favourite material and place some of it inside a large, clear plastic bottle or cardboard tube.

5. Glue or tape the lids onto the bottles and try out the shaker-rattle 'n' roller. Sing the following song to the tune of 'Jelly on a Plate':

   Shake, shake, shake (x2)

   Rattle, rattle, rattle, rattle

   And then try a roll.

What's in it for the children?

Children can explore sounds and gain independence by choosing their favourite materials. They will also learn to work cooperatively with partners and in larger groups.

Taking it forward

- Ask the children to find a partner. Invite them to roll their bottle or tube to each other and listen to the sound. Extend this to the whole group sitting in a circle and sharing each other's 'rattle and roll' sounds by rolling the shakers across the ring.

- Challenge the children to identify the different rattle sounds with their eyes closed or wearing a blindfold.

✚ Health & Safety

Remind children not to put any of the filling materials in their mouths.

Great guiros

Scraping and scratching in time to the beat

What you need:

- A selection of musical instruments to scrape, such as guiros and cabasas
- Frog guiros (optional)
- A selection of recycled items to scrape such as ridged plastic bottles, corrugated card, sandpaper and textured fabric
- Wooden blocks (optional)
- A recording device (e.g. a tablet)

What's in it for the children?

Children will explore lots of different scraping sounds, inside and outside, and use them to play patterns and rhythms.

Taking it forward

- Wrap sandpaper or corrugated cardboard around wooden blocks to create scrapers. Scrape two blocks together. Show the children a video of 'Sandpaper Ballet' by Leroy Anderson, available online.
- Show them the performance of 'Brooms' from the theatre event STOMP, available online.
- Let the children use tablets to record each other as they discover new sounds.

✚ Health & Safety

Let children wear gloves when exploring scraping sounds outside.

What to do:

1. Go on a 'scratchy walk' and invite the children to find out how many different scratchy sounds they can discover inside. They can try scraping furniture, clothes and whiteboards with their fingers.

2. Go outside and run a stick along a wooden fence, brick walls or pavement. Explore sweeping sounds using brushes. Try scraping two found objects together. Record all the different sounds.

3. Ask the children to rub their hands together and listen to the sound. Invite them to copy some rubbing rhythm patterns.

4. Let the children experiment with some guiros or cabasas. Try some frog guiros and create a frog chorus.

5. Show the children how to play the guiros using an up and down movement. Play along to some music with a strong beat.

6. You can sing the following song to the tune of 'London's Burning':

   Scrape the guiros, scrape the guiros,

   Up and down, side to side.

   Scritch, scratch, scribble, scrape,

   Here's the sound, the guiros make.

7. Use pencils or metal spoons to scrape and scratch some recycled items and explore a variety of sounds.

Knock on wood

Having a rave with some claves

What you need:

- Pairs of claves, enough for each child
- A collection of wood blocks and other wooden musical instruments
- Music with a strong beat

Top tip

If you don't have enough claves for all the children, use pairs of pencils or short, thin pieces of wood.

What to do:

1. Ask the children to sit in a circle and begin with some echo clapping (see 'Stamp, clap, click, tap', page 17).

2. Place a pair of claves in front of each child. Encourage the children to pick up the claves on a signal, one in each hand, and hold them like candles on their knees. This is called the 'claves circle'.

3. Invite the children to copy what you play and try some echo tapping using the claves.

4. Choose one rhythm pattern and ask the children to join in as you repeat it over and over like an ostinato (see 'Ostinato loops', page 21). Tell the children this is called a 'claves groove' and let them choose different rhythms to repeat.

5. Try playing a steady beat on the claves and other wooden instruments to some music with a strong pulse.

6. Show the children some different ways to play the claves: end to end, side to side, on the floor, and so on.

7. Enjoy a 'claves rave' and let the children play whatever they want or improvise using the claves along to some dance music.

What's in it for the children?

Playing the claves will develop children's coordination and fine motor skills at the same time as learning more about beat and rhythm.

Taking it forward

- Invite children to take turns leading some echo tapping. Show them a performance of 'Music for Pieces of Wood' by Steve Reich, available online.

- Play 'Stop, don't, tap that one' from 'Repeat after me', page 18, using claves.

- Show the children pictures and videos of clapsticks, a traditional Australian Aboriginal instrument.

✚ Health & Safety

Show children how to hold the claves correctly so that they don't hit their fingers when they play them.

Tapping times two

Lots more rhythm games

What you need:

- A recording device (e.g. a tablet)

- A selection of untuned percussion instruments such as claves, castanets, wood blocks, coconuts, cowbells and triangles (see 'Useful resources', page 5)

- Recycled instruments such as pairs of plastic yoghurt pots, lids of washing liquid bottles or aerosols, wooden spoons and cardboard tubes

What's in it for the children?

Children will explore different tapping sounds and play some rhythm games to increase their physical coordination and rhythmic skills.

Taking it forward

- Make your own castanets (see 'Music workshop', page 42). Watch some traditional flamenco music videos featuring castanets.

- Choose two different instruments and invite the children to play them together. Ask one child to play a slow beat while the other plays twice as fast.

- Show the children some examples of tap dancing.

- Create a guessing game by recording the different sounds and asking children to identify the instrument.

What to do:

1. Start with some echo clapping and tapping (see 'Knock on wood', page 30).

2. Go around the setting with a small group of children and try tapping different surfaces to discover new sounds. The children could use their fingertips and knuckles. Record the sounds.

3. Let the children explore tapping sounds using a selection of untuned percussion instruments or recycled materials (see 'What you need', page 5).

4. Ask the children to sit in a circle and place an instrument in front of each child. Let them explore the different sounds they can make. Move the instruments around so children can try a new one.

5. Sing the following song with the children to the tune of 'Here We Go Round the Mulberry Bush':

   Tap together, hear the sound,

   Tap together, change the sound,

   Tap together, round and round.

   Tap, tap, tap, together.

6. Play a game of 'Tap in the gap' (see 'All in the name', page 20). Ask the children to tap their instrument four times and then count to four to create a gap before the next four taps. Can they take turns to tap a rhythm in the gap?

Drumming drives

Exploring the world of drums

What you need:

- A selection of different tambourines, tambours and hand drums, one for each child
- A large sharing or gathering drum

Top tip

If you haven't got enough drums for every child, use large biscuit or sweet tins.

What's in it for the children?

Children will be able to play simple rhythms on a variety of drums, on their own and together in a group.

Taking it forward

- Try some of the rhythm games in 'Knock on wood', page 30, and 'Tapping times two', page 31.
- Make your own drums! See 'Music workshop', page 42.
- Display a collection of hand drums from around the world, such as djembes, darbuka, mridangam, tabla, congas, bongos and bodhráns. Compare the sounds. If you don't have access to the drums, play snippets online. Show the children on a map where each drum originates from.

What to do:

1. Ask the children to sit in a drumming circle and start with a game of 'Pass the drum' using one tambourine or hand drum. Sing the following song to the tune of 'Wheels on the Bus'. The child holding the drum on the word 'Stop' can play or improvise whatever they like on the drum:

   Pass the drum around the ring,

   Round the ring, as you sing,

   Pass the drum around the ring,

   Stop and play…

2. Provide each child with a drum. Ask them to pick the drums up and hold them silently. On an agreed signal (see 'Start and stop', page 38) let the children all start and stop playing together. Practise lots of times.

3. Try playing quietly, loudly, fast, slowly and one at a time. Can they echo a simple rhythm pattern all together?

4. Place one large drum or a set of smaller drums in the middle of the circle and choose a group of four or five children to come and play together. Sing their names to gather them around the drums. Ask them to echo a rhythm pattern on the drum or drums, on their own and all together.

Playing with pitch

Playing with high and low sounds

What you need:

- A selection of tuned percussion instruments such as chime bars, xylophones, glockenspiels, kalimbas, etc. (see 'Useful resources', page 5)
- Small whiteboards and pens
- Five empty, clear glass bottles or jars
- Water and food colouring
- A metal or wooden spoon

What's in it for the children?

Pitch can be a confusing concept for young children. Experiencing it physically through actions and making up their own patterns will help children begin to understand it.

Taking it forward

- Add a middle sound ('m') and include it in the pitch patterns.
- Make a water xylophone by filling five glass bottles with different amounts of coloured water. Tap them with a metal or wooden spoon, listening to the different sounds.
- Arrange the bottles in order from low to high pitch and number them one to five.
- Let the children make up their own patterns using the bottles. Can they write some patterns for others to play?

✚ Health & Safety

Remind children to take care using glass bottles in case of breakages.

What to do:

1. Sing a song to introduce high and low movements. Sing it slowly to the tune of 'Hot Cross Buns', stretching hands up high and touching toes along to the lyrics:

   High, low, freeze,

   High, low, still.

   Will you hear the changing pitches?

   Yes we will.

2. Demonstrate high and low sounds on any tuned instrument. Introduce the children to the term 'pitch' (see 'Musical terms', page 5).

3. Play a game of 'High, low, up and down we go'. Play a high sound and the children stretch up high to reach the sky. Play a low sound and they bend down low to touch their toes. Let the children take turns to lead the game.

4. Play the children the movement 'Characters with Long Ears' from the 'The Carnival of the Animals' by Camille Saint-Saëns. Listen to the contrasting high and low sounds.

5. Invite pairs of children to explore the different sounds they can make on tuned percussion instruments.

6. Write the letters 'h' and 'l' in a sequence on a whiteboard. Point to the letters one after another, encouraging the children to play high or low notes as you point to each letter.

Pentatonic patterns

Making up some tunes using five notes

What you need:

- A xylophone
- A selection of tuned percussion instruments such as chime bars, hand chimes, glockenspiels and Boomwhackers® (see 'Useful resources', page 5)
- Small whiteboards and pens, or paper to write on

Top tip

Show the children videos of people playing the balafon, a West African xylophone made with gourds, and the gamelan, a percussion ensemble from Indonesia.

What's in it for the children?

Children will benefit from lots of opportunities to experiment freely on tuned instruments, holding beaters and coordinating their movements.

Taking it forward

- Try some echo patterns. Use the two notes, G and E, as used in echo singing (see 'Hear me hum', page 11). Use different tuned instruments such as chime bars, hand chimes and Boomwhackers®.
- Challenge the children to try to notate their two-note patterns and write them on whiteboards.

✚ Health & Safety

Remind children to play the instruments carefully and without too much force.

What to do:

1. Remind the children about high and low sounds (see 'Playing with pitch', page 33). Stand a xylophone up like a ladder with the long bars at the bottom. Can the children hear the difference between the low sounds at the bottom and the high sounds at the top?

2. Ask the children to crouch down. As you play the notes of the ladder from the bottom to the top, invite them to grow gradually taller.

3. Take the B and F bars off the xylophone until you are left with a five-note or pentatonic scale: C, D, E, G, and A (see 'Musical terms' page 5). Let the children improvise or make up patterns using the five notes.

4. Invite the children to play together on different tuned instruments. If they all use the pentatonic scale, it will sound great.

5. Sing a song with the children to the tune of '1, 2, 3, 4, 5, Once I Caught a Fish Alive':

   1, 2, 3 4 5,

   I can play a pattern.

   C, D, E, G, A

   Pentatonic pattern.

6. Write some patterns using the letter names for the children to play. Try C, C, G, C or C, D, E, E, D, C. Can they write their own patterns?

Metal machines

Using metal sounds to make musical machines

What you need:

- A selection of metal instruments such as jingle bells, cowbells, cymbals, hand cymbals, cabasa, agogô bells, triangles, glockenspiels and chime bars

- A large picture of a robot or machine

- Paints and brushes

- Recycled materials, such as cardboard boxes, yoghurt pots, etc.

- Glue or tape

What's in it for the children?

Children will learn about how to create sound effects and explore lots of different metal instruments.

Taking it forward

- Invite a group of children to paint a picture of a robot or make one using recycled materials. Choose different metal sounds to make for each part of the machine.

- Show the children videos of 'The Typewriter' by Leroy Anderson or the Metranomes Steel Orchestra, available online.

- Let the children experiment with a drum machine app.

 ### Health & Safety

Some metal instruments are quite heavy and need careful handling.

What to do:

1. Sit the children in a circle and place an instrument in front of each child. Ask them to pick them up and hold them silently.

2. Can they work out how to make a sound with their instrument? Demonstrate techniques where necessary. Talk to the children about shaking, ringing, tapping, and scraping.

3. Ask the children, 'What have all the instruments got in common?' (Answer: they're all made of metal!)

4. Invite the children to take turns to introduce their instrument to the group, name it, model how to play it and listen carefully to the sound it makes.

5. On an agreed signal (see 'Start and stop', page 38) let them all start to play at the same time and try to stop together.

6. Sing this adaptation of 'The Music Man', including different metal instruments:

   I am the metal man,

   I come from far away and I can play.

   What can you play?

   Tria-tria-triangle, triangle, triangle…

7. Explain that you are going to use the instruments to make the sounds of a 'Metal Man'. Show the children the robot picture and invite them to select sounds for it using the metal instruments available.

Top tip ⭐

If you haven't got enough metal instruments, use kitchenware.

Whistling wonders

Exploring wind instruments together

What you need:

- Lots of small plastic bottles
- A selection of toy wind instruments such as whistles and party blowers
- Various wind instruments, for example, tin whistles, panpipes, swanee whistles, harmonicas, recorders and ocarinas
- Antibacterial wipes

What's in it for the children?

Children will learn about new ways to make musical sounds using wind instruments from all around the world.

Taking it forward

- Listen to some wind instruments online and discuss similarities and differences.

- Introduce some sound science (see 'Playing with sounds', page 44). Explain that wind instruments make a sound by making a tube of air vibrate.

- Talk about how size affects pitch. For example, explain that long tubes or big instruments make low sounds, while short tubes or small instruments make high sounds.

Health & Safety

Make sure you wipe instruments with antibacterial wipes between uses.

What to do:

1. Try some whistling and let the children have a go. If you cannot whistle, play music which includes whistling such as 'Whistle While You Work' from Walt Disney's *Snow White* or 'Finnish Whistler' by Roger Whittaker.

2. Show the children how to blow across the top of plastic bottles to create a sound. Who can create the longest or loudest sound?

3. Let the children explore blowing with a selection of wind instruments.

4. Create a class wind band. Place a wind instrument in front of each child. Go around the circle and invite each child to demonstrate their sound one at a time. Sing the song to the tune of 'We Can Play on the Big Bass Drum':

   Oh I can play on the [tin whistle]

   And this is the way I do it.

   Toot, toot, toot on the [tin whistle]

   Listen to the music.

5. Play all together using some starting and stopping signals (see 'Start and stop', page 38).

Pluck, strum and twang

Finding out how strings make different sounds

What you need:

- A loop of stretchy rope or elastic
- A ukelele or guitar (or another string instrument)
- Empty tissue and shoe boxes
- Elastic bands

Top tip

Invite a string player to visit and demonstrate their instrument to the children. Alternatively, listen online to string instruments from around the world such as banjos, sitars, mandolins, balalaika, oud and kora.

What's in it for the children?

Children will experience playing strings and learn about how string instruments make sounds. Plucking strings also supports the development of fine motor skills.

Taking it forward

- Make a box guitar using a tissue box or a shoe box. If you're using a shoe box, cut an oval sound hole in the lid. Let each child select three different-sized elastic bands and stretch them over the empty box width ways so they vibrate over the hole. Do the bands make different notes?
- Explain that the instruments create sounds by making the strings vibrate. The sound hole in the instrument amplifies the sound.

What to do:

1. Sit in a circle with all the children holding onto a loop of stretchy rope or elastic. Try some rowing movements in and out as you sing 'Row, Row, Row Your Boat'.

2. Ask half of the children to let go of the elastic so that the string 'twangs'. Can they hear the sound?

3. Show the children a ukulele or guitar and invite them to listen as you pluck the strings. Try turning the tuning pegs and plucking again - can they hear the pitch change? Invite them to imitate the 'twang' sound with their voices.

4. Sing a song using a rhythm played on the open strings (without placing your hand on the frets). Pluck the strings one at a time and sing 'I can sing with the open string'.

5. Strum all the strings together. Let the children take turns to pluck or strum the strings.

6. Play the open strings on the ukulele: G, C, E, A. Try this simple chant as a mnemonic device:

   Go Count Each Ant,

   1, 2, 3, 4,

   Go Count Each Ant,

   Then count some more.

7. Demonstrate the chord C major on the ukulele. Put your left-hand ring finger on the third fret of the 'A' string. Use this chord to accompany the children singing 'Row, Row, Row Your Boat'.

Start and stop

Practising starting and stopping sounds

What you need:

- Green and red circles of cardboard
- A selection of untuned percussion instruments such as claves, castanets, wood blocks, coconuts cowbells and triangles (see 'Useful resources', page 5)

Top tip

Practise the children's start and stop hand signals all together at first so they are familiar with the movement.

What's in it for the children?

Conducting using simple hand signals helps children begin to select and organise musical sounds.

Taking it forward

- Start and stop one instrument at a time. Listen to the different sounds.

- Invite the children to take turns walking around the circle choosing instruments to listen to. Encourage them to say the name of the different instruments they are choosing to hear.

- Watch some clips of conductors conducting orchestras online.

What to do:

1. Ask the children to find a space to stand in. Show them the green and red circles, which represent 'start' and 'stop' traffic lights. Invite them to move when the green circle is held up and stop when they see the red.

2. Sit the children in a circle. Explain that you are going to use conducting hand signals to start and stop musical sounds.

3. Show them the 'start' signal by opening your hands, palm upwards. Invite the children to make a noise with their hands – clapping, rubbing, tapping, etc.

4. Show them the 'stop' signal by closing your hands into fists as though you are holding onto handlebars. How quickly can they stop the sounds?

5. Practise starting and stopping the sounds. Remind everyone to keep watching your hands! Sing the song to the tune of 'I Hear Thunder':

   Can you start? We can start.

   Can you stop? We can stop.

   Play a new sound.

   Pass it around.

   Can you stop? We can stop!

6. Place an instrument in front of each child. Ask the children to pick them up and wait for the signal to start playing. Try starting and stopping the instruments. Vary the amount of time the children are playing. Can you catch them out by stopping very quickly?

7. Invite the children to take turns using the start and stop signals. The conductor can stand up so all the children in the circle can see their hands.

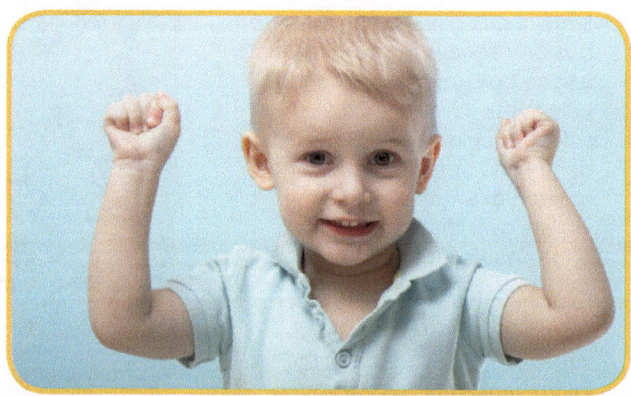

Discovering dynamics

Exploring quiet and loud sounds

What you need:

- A selection of musical instruments, enough for each child

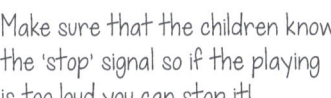

Top tip ⭐

Make sure that the children know the 'stop' signal so if the playing is too loud you can stop it!

What's in it for the children?

Children will show increased confidence and coordination in playing musical instruments and extend their knowledge of musical terminology.

Taking it forward

- Invite the children to take turns conducting loud and quiet sounds using their hands.
- Play 'Creepy crescendo'. Invite one child to be the conductor. Ask them to choose a child to start playing, then walk around the circle adding instruments until everyone is playing together. What happens to the sound? Now reverse it and the sound grows quieter (a diminuendo)!
- Listen to the change in dynamics in 'It's Oh So Quiet' sung by Björk.

✚ Health & Safety

Remind children to take care when producing loud sounds so that they don't damage the instruments.

What to do:

1. Start by creating a silence. Ask the children to make a quiet humming sound together, then use the 'stop' hand signal to stop the sound and wait (see 'Start and stop', page 38). Listen to the silence.

2. Introduce the musical term 'dynamics' to describe loud and quiet (see 'Musical terms', page 5). Can the children name some loud and quiet sounds?

3. Challenge the children to play their instruments very quietly. Try all playing quietly together. Use open hands close together to signal quiet sounds.

4. Go around the circle and invite each child to play their instrument as loudly as they can. Try all playing loudly together. Use open hands far apart to signal loud sounds.

5. Ask the children to switch between loud and quiet sounds as you sing 'Three Quiet Mice':

   Three quiet mice, three quiet mice,
   Listen to the sound, listen to the sound.
   Now change the sound to playing loud,
   And everyone's playing in a crowd,
   And play as though you're very proud,
   Three noisy mice.

6. Invite the children to create a crescendo (a sound which gradually gets louder) following your hand signals. Start with open hands close together and slowly move your hands far apart.

Leader of the band

Taking turns to choose and change sounds

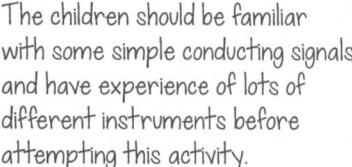

What you need:

- A selection of musical instruments, enough for each child

Top tip ⭐

The children should be familiar with some simple conducting signals and have experience of lots of different instruments before attempting this activity.

➕ Health & Safety

Remind children to play the instruments carefully and without too much force.

What to do:

1. Place a musical instrument in front of each child in the circle. Allow time for the children to explore the sounds the instrument makes. Then invite them to change places and try out a new sound.

2. Let the children take turns to be the conductor or leader of the band, using start and stop signals to conduct the sounds (see 'Start and stop', page 38).

3. Invite them to change the dynamics using ideas from 'Discovering dynamics', page 39.

4. Make up some new hand signs to change tempo and explore playing the instruments quickly and slowly (see 'Musical terms', page 5). For example, try flapping open hands up and down, fast and slowly, to vary the tempo.

5. Play some music with varying tempos, such as 'Kangaroos' from 'The Carnival of the Animals' by Camille Saint-Saëns.

6. Find some instruments that play long sustained sounds, such as triangles, cymbals and chime bars. Compare them with instruments that play short sounds, like wood blocks and drums. Play a long and short sound pattern for the children to copy.

7. Choose a child to be conductor and let them pick one instrument or group of instruments to listen to. Can they use their conducting skills to choose and change the tempo and dynamics of the sounds?

What's in it for the children?

Children will gain independence by choosing which instruments to listen to and changing how they play.

Taking it forward

- Play a game of 'Spot the conductor'. Ask the children to sit in a circle and ask for a volunteer to leave the room. Choose a conductor to lead the band. Everybody mimes playing an instrument that the conductor selects. Invite the volunteer to return and stand in the middle of the circle. When they are not looking, the conductor changes the instrument and the rest of the group copy. The volunteer has three guesses to identify the conductor.

Music workshop

Making DIY instruments

What you need:

- Scissors, glue, a hole punch, sticky tape, split pins and a stapler
- Strips of cardboard and bottle tops
- Balloons and empty cardboard or sweet tins
- Empty round, wooden cheese boxes, wooden spoons, beads and shoelaces
- Paper plates, rice, bells and coloured wool or ribbon
- Cardboard tubes, paper, elastic bands, foil, wooden spoons and rice
- Art materials to decorate the instruments
- A recording device such as a tablet

What to do:

1. Set up a music workshop with lots of recycled materials, tools and simple instructions. Let the children choose an instrument to make in the workshop.

2. **Clicking castanets:** Provide the children with pre-cut strips of cardboard, 5 cm by 11 cm. Help them to score and fold the card in half with a 1 cm wide spine. Stick a bottle top onto the inside of each rectangle so that they tap together when the card is folded.

3. **Balloon drums:** Stretch an empty balloon over a tin and secure with tape.

4. **Rattle drums:** Thread a bead onto each end of a shoelace. Tie the shoelace around the neck of a wooden spoon. Cut gaps in the edge of a wooden cheese box and stick the top of the spoon inside the cheese box, sealing it with glue. Twist the handle between both hands so the beads create a rattle sound.

5. **Tambourines:** Stick two paper plates together, adding a handful of rice inside before sealing. Punch holes around the edge and thread small pieces of coloured wool or ribbon through them. Fasten bells onto the wool or ribbon.

6. **Rainsticks:** Cover one end of a cardboard tube securely with a circle of paper and an elastic band. Fold a length of foil into a 1 cm wide strip and shape it into a spiral by wrapping it around the handle of a wooden spoon. Carefully remove the foil spiral from the spoon and put it inside the tube. Add a handful of rice and seal the open end of the tube.

Top tip

Use a glue gun to make the instruments last longer.

What's in it for the children?

Children will learn to follow instructions and think about the components of an instrument. They can get creative by choosing what to make and playing their instruments together.

Taking it forward

- Create a band with the DIY instruments and perform together. Use the instruments to accompany well-known songs.

- Let the children decorate the instruments to personalise them.

- Record the children playing their instruments and play it back. Can they recognise the different sounds?

 **Health & Safety**

Remind children to take care handling 'tools' in the workshop.

Playing with sounds

Finding out how different sounds are made

What you need:

- A blindfold
- A musical instrument
- A water tray or bowl
- A pebble
- A large drum
- Rice
- A soft toy
- Paper or plastic cups
- String
- Scissors

What's in it for the children?

Children will investigate the science behind how we hear sounds, and the different ways that instruments make sounds.

Taking it forward

- Make home-made telephones for the children to phone a friend with. Using scissors, poke a hole in the bottom of two paper or plastic cups and thread through a length of string. Tie knots in each end and pull the string taut. Ask the children to try them out with a partner.

- Search online for the Chrome Music Lab and let the children experiment with different sound-making tools.

Health & Safety

Take care using scissors or cutting tools.

What to do:

1. Begin with a song to the tune of 'In and Out the Dusty Bluebells':

   Pluck the string and tap the drum.
   Can you hear our voices hum?
   Blow the pipe and shake the bell,
   Voices whisper, voices yell.

2. Play a game of 'Sounds around'. Sit the children in a circle. Ask for a volunteer to wear a blindfold and sit in the middle. Point at another child to use their voice or play a musical instrument. Can the listener identify where the sound is coming from? Move the sound around and try again.

3. Stand around a water tray. Invite a child to drop a pebble into the water and watch the ripples as they spread. Explain to the children that sound travels in waves through the air.

4. Place a few grains of rice on the top of a drum. Invite a child to tap the drum and watch the rice jump up and down. The top of the drum vibrates and creates a sound wave. Relate this to vibrating strings in string instruments and columns of air in wind instruments.

5. Play a game of 'Sound detectives'. Sit the children in a circle. Ask for a volunteer to leave the room while another child hides a soft toy somewhere. Invite the children to guide the detective to the hiding place using loud clapping (hot) and quiet clapping (cold).

Design your own instrument
Building unique instruments

What you need:

- A selection of musical instruments
- Paper and pencils
- Recycled materials including different-sized plastic bottles and lids, cardboard tubes with metal bases, plastic tubes, etc.
- Additional extras: elastic bands, metal bells, textured paper, different fillings (rice, lentils, etc.)
- Tools: scissors, a stapler, string, sticky tape, split pins, glue, etc.

What's in it for the children?

Children will have experience of using recycled materials to make a variety of sounds and construct musical instruments.

Taking it forward

- Ask the children to sit in a circle and take turns to demonstrate their handmade instruments.
- Show children videos of orchestras which use recycled instruments.
- Organise the instruments into a DIY band. Invite parents and carers to a concert to hear the children play together in the band.

✚ Health & Safety

Remind children to take care handling tools in the workshop.

What to do:

1. Sit the children in a circle and place a selection of musical instruments in the centre.
2. The children can take turns to pick up an instrument and find out how it works – tap, shake, scrape, rattle, pluck, etc. How many different ways can it make a sound?
3. Explain to the children that they can design and make their own musical instrument in the music workshop. Provide paper and pencils so they can draw their design ideas first.
4. Lay all the recycled materials and tools out for the children (keeping any sharp items out of reach). Allow the children lots of time to experiment and test their ideas in the music workshop. Take a look at the ideas in 'Music workshop', page 42.
5. Challenge them to create an instrument that makes sounds in more than one way.
6. Make up a chant that incorporates their homemade instruments, for example:

   Tap on the box, tap on the tin,
   Shake the bottle, fast and slow.
   Rattle the tin, rattle the trays,
   Make some sounds, high and low.

Top tip ⭐

Assist the children by demonstrating how to join parts together or helping to solve construction problems.

The recording studio

Exploring simple music technology

What you need:

- An electronic keyboard
- A recording device (e.g. a tablet) and camera
- Headphones, a microphone and a music stand
- A stage block or mat, or cushions and masking tape
- A selection of musical instruments
- Notation cards or graphic sounds cards (see 'Notation notes', page 49, or 'Duos, trios and quirky quartets', page 58)

What to do:

1. Set up a role play recording studio in your setting, using a corner or table area. Provide an electronic keyboard for the children to explore new sounds.
2. Show them how to use simple recording equipment (such as a tablet) and cameras so they can record sounds and add visuals in the studio.
3. Let them dress up in headphones and use a microphone to act the part. Do they need a music stand to put their graphic sound cards or notation cards on?
4. Provide a stage block or mat, or mark out an area using masking tape and comfy cushions for them to practise their performances. The children can work on their own or with others.
5. Encourage the children to use their voices, body percussion, musical instruments, including DIY ones (see 'Music Workshop' page 42 and 'Design your own instrument', page 45). Children could record themselves playing one of the other activities in this book.

What's in it for the children?

Recording music is a great way to keep records of the music making in your setting. It also gives children an opportunity to experiment with technology.

Taking it forward

- Search online for 'BBC Bring the Noise' and start experimenting with music technology by playing some games.
- Play some examples of electronic music. You can find playlists of electronic music for children on music streaming websites.
- Find some nursery rhyme apps for children and invite them to sing along , or visit the BBC Teach 'School Radio' website.

✚ Health & Safety

Make sure children know how to use the equipment safely.

Be a sound sorter

Sorting instrument sounds into sets

What you need:

- A selection of musical instruments, enough for each child
- Four different-coloured hula hoops
- Laminated labels for each group of instruments: wood, metal, skin or plastic

Top tip

When handing out the instruments try not to place two of the same next to each other.

What's in it for the children?

Children will be able to identify matching sounds and sort instruments into groups according to an agreed criteria. This will also help their understanding of different materials.

Taking it forward

- Try sorting the instruments in different ways such as how they are played (shaken, scraped, tapped or plucked); tuned or untuned; or according to size. Are there any instruments that can be played in more than one way? Tambourines can be tapped and shaken. How will the children sort them?
- Play a game of 'Musical snap'. Invite a child to hide behind a screen and play one or more instruments. Ask the children in the circle to listen, identify and copy the sounds they hear.

What to do:

1. Sit the children in a circle and place an instrument in front of each child. Use the conducting signals in 'Start and stop', page 38, to practise playing together.

2. Listen to the sounds of the different instruments one by one. Sing 'Here We Come, One By One', to the tune of 'Rain, Rain, Go Away', as each child takes a turn at playing their instrument around the circle:

   Here we come, one by one,

   Listen to the sounds.

   Taking turns, one by one,

   As we move around.

3. Find matching sounds by playing 'Join in with me, 1, 2, 3'. Invite one child to play an instrument and anybody with the same instrument can join in after the count.

4. Place the four hoops in the middle of the circle. Explain that you are going to sort the instruments according to what they are made of: wood, metal, skin or plastic. (Skin refers to drums and other percussion instruments; explain to children that they used to be made from animal hide but are now usually made from synthetic materials.) Make laminated labels for each group.

5. Invite all the children with an instrument made of wood to stand up and play their sounds together. Ask them to carefully place the instruments into one of the hoops.

6. Repeat with the other groups of instruments.

Sound sandwiches

Organising sounds into simple structures

What you need:

- A selection of musical instruments, enough for each child
- Four different-coloured hula hoops
- A card with the letters 'ABA' written on it
- A recording device, e.g. a tablet (optional)

What's in it for the children?

Children will begin to compose by selecting sounds and organising them into simple forms or structures.

Taking it forward

- Try some 'Solo sandwiches'. Invite one child from the metal group (A) and one child from the skin group (B) to stand inside their hoops. Can they play their instruments to create a sound sandwich?

- Record the children playing and listen back. Can they hear the change in sounds? Discuss ways to improve the sound sandwiches.

- Sort the instruments according to how they are played and try some sound sandwiches. For example, A = shake and B = scrape or A = quiet and B = loud.

What to do:

1. Sort the instruments into four groups – wood, metal, skin and plastic (see 'Be a sound sorter', page 47) and place them into the hoops, using one hoop for each group.

2. Divide the children into four groups and invite them, one group at a time, to sit around a hoop and select an instrument.

3. Listen to each group of instruments and talk about the different sounds or timbres of the instruments (see 'Musical terms', page 5).

4. Explain that they are going to make a sound sandwich using the groups. Invite the wood instruments to play (representing the bread), the metal instruments (the filling) and then the wood instruments again (the bread again).

5. Introduce the letters ABA to illustrate the structure of the sound sandwich.

6. Invite the children to choose a different make-up for the sandwich, e.g. A = skin, B = plastic, A = skin.

7. Sing a simple chant with the children:

   Make a sound sandwich, (x2)

   Choose the filling with care.

   Make a sound sandwich. (x2)

8. Sing the nursery rhyme 'Twinkle Twinkle Little Star' and point out the ABA form. Listen to some music which demonstrates ABA such as 'Galop' by Dmitri Kabalevsky, 'Norwegian Dance No. 2, by Edvard Grieg or 'Trumpeter's Lullaby' by Leroy Anderson.

Notation notes

Different ways to write down sounds

What you need:

- Musical instruments, enough for each child
- Strips of card
- Felt-tip pens
- Hand puppets and rhythm cards

What's in it for the children?

Children will begin to use different ways to notate their music for each other to play.

Taking it forward

- Try some pitch notation using 'h', 'm' and 'l' to signify high, medium and low sounds (see, 'Playing with pitch', page 34). Play three contrasting chime bars or notes on a xylophone.

- Instead of 'h', 'm' and 'l', use dots and lines to signify high, medium and low. High = a dot above a line, middle = a dot with a line through it and low = a dot under a line.

- Search online for examples of graphic notation, and show the children the creative ways that people notate music.

- Introduce simple rhythm notation using hand puppets called Ben and Bessie. Ben holds a rhythm card with a ♩ and Bessie holds a card with a ♫. Ask the children to clap once for Ben and twice for Bessie as they say the names. Let them use the notated rhythm cards to create rhythm patterns.

What to do:

1. Ask the children to help sort the instruments into four groups (see 'Be a sound sorter', page 47).

2. Explain that they are going to experiment with different ways to notate or write down sounds.

3. Invent some symbols to represent each group, for instance X = wood, O = skin, Δ = metal, and ∞ = plastic. Use these symbols to write down some ABA patterns (see 'Sound sandwiches', page 48), e.g. X ∞ X.

4. Try some different structures, e.g. ABABAB. Let the children perform the music from the notation, e.g. Δ O Δ O Δ O.

5. Make graphic sound cards representing different ways to play sounds, for instance, ● ● ● ● = four taps, VVVV = four shakes, //// = four scrapes, xxxx = four rattles, OOOO = four rings.

6. Invite the children to write their own patterns on cards for others to read and play.

Top tip ⭐

Make a set of laminated cards with selected sound symbols on to use again and again.

Sound effects station

Creating sound effects using voices and instruments

What you need:

- A selection of musical instruments
- A variety of recycled materials: plastic trays, plastic lids, wooden spoons, newspaper, sandpaper, etc.
- Access to recorded sound effects online, available at www.freesfx.com

Top tip

Try not to be too prescriptive with ideas for sound effects. Allow the children to use their imaginations.

What to do:

1. Sit quietly and invite the children to listen carefully to the sounds around them. Make a list of the sounds they heard.

2. Try again and this time, while the children are listening, discreetly make a quiet sound such as scratching or tapping a table with one finger. Stop after a minute and see if the children noticed the extra sound.

3. What did the children think the secret sound was? (A mouse, clock, rain, etc.). Reveal what it was.

4. Talk to the children about sound effects. Play some examples of sound effects online. You could play a 'sound effects bingo' game to practise identifying sounds.

5. Place a selection of instruments and recycled materials in the circle. Brainstorm ideas for sound effects for the ticking of a clock, footsteps, a door opening, knocking on a door, a train, wind, water, waves, etc.

6. Sing a song to the tune of 'If You're Happy and You Know It':

   Make a sound like a step...

   Make a sound like a bell...

   Make a sound like a clock...

   Does it go tick-tock?

   Make a sound like a clock...

   Can you tell?

7. Set up a sound effects station and let the children experiment using voices, instruments and other materials.

What's in it for the children?

Children will learn to create sound effects using a variety of materials and instruments to make a soundscape for a story, picture or song.

Taking it forward

- Challenge pairs or groups of children to make as many different sounds as they can with one item, such as a newspaper or a saucepan lid.

- Watch a cartoon with the sound turned down. Can the children suggest where they could add sound effects? Choose instruments or recycled materials to create some sound effects for the cartoon.

Tell me a story

Using sound effects to tell a story

What you need:

- A selection of musical instruments
- A variety of recycled materials: plastic trays, tin lids, wooden spoons, newspaper, sandpaper, etc.
- Finger puppets or soft toys
- A favourite picture book (optional)

Top tip

If the children struggle to come up with new story ideas, try basing it on a well-known traditional story.

What's in it for the children?

Children will be able to use their imagination to create sound effects and motifs for characters and events in their own story.

Taking it forward

- Can the children tell the story just using the sound effects?
- Add sound effects to a favourite picture book. Let the children use their voices, body percussion and instruments to create the sounds.
- Listen to a recording of 'Peter and the Wolf' by Sergei Prokofiev, in which the characters are represented by different instruments.

What to do:

1. Recap some of the sound effect ideas from 'Sound effects station', page 50.

2. In small groups, make up a story. For example, 'Once upon a time there was a… '. Introduce a character using a finger puppet or soft toy. What is their name? What sounds could the character make?

3. Go around the group and invite the children to make some sound effects using recycled materials, instruments or body percussion. Choose a child to make the sound every time the character is mentioned as you tell the story together.

4. Invent other characters to join the story. Create a sound effect or musical motif (a recurring sound) to represent the new characters.

5. Decide on a setting for the story, such as going for a walk and finding a haunted house. Make up sound effects for the setting, such as walking, opening doors, creaky floorboards and climbing upstairs. How will the story end?

6. Tell the story again: the children should try to remember all the sound effects.

Sound sculptures

Making a sound installation

What you need:

- A solid structure to build your sculpture on, such as a tree, a climbing frame or an empty a clothes rack
- Hooks, garden wire or string to attach items
- Lots of different metal, wooden, plastic and natural sound sources, such as spoons, sieves, pans, keys, tins, rulers, pencils, coconuts, shells, etc.

Top tip

This can be used as part of continuous provision by changing the items attached to the sculpture.

What's in it for the children?

Children will learn to work together, cooperate in small groups and develop their creativity.

Taking it forward

- Challenge the children to use the sound sculpture to accompany a story, song or game.
- Show the children videos of sound sculptures online. For example, the 'Singing Ringing Tree' in Burnley, England, or the 'Sea Organ' in Zadar, Croatia.

✚ Health & Safety

Take care handling any sharp objects.

What to do:

1. Explain to the children that they are going to go outside and create a sound sculpture to use to make music. Talk about a suitable base for the sculpture such as a tree, branch or frame.

2. Experiment with items to hang on the structure. Can they describe the different sounds they make, such as ringing, clattering, tapping, dinging, chiming and blowing?

3. Fix some hooks into the structure for the children to hang different items on.

4. Show the children how to attach string or wire onto the sound sources so they can hang the items up on the hooks.

5. In small groups, let the children take turns to select different items to hang on the structure and make sounds.

6. Provide a box of different items for the children to try out each week so the sound sculpture changes and develops.

Stormy weather

Using sounds to create a picture of a storm

What you need:

- A selection of musical instruments
- DIY instruments (see 'Music workshop', page 42)
- A recording device (e.g. a tablet)

Top tip

If you haven't got enough instruments for each child to have one, use voices and body percussion as well.

What's in it for the children?

Children will learn to use their imagination to compose soundscapes linked to different environments.

Taking it forward

- Let the children take turns to create the storm by starting and stopping the instruments around the circle. Can they hear the sound grow louder and quieter (see 'Discovering dynamics', page 39)?

- Choose a different scenario to create using dynamics, such as a fireworks display.

- Record the children's performances and listen back to the soundscapes.

- Play the children some music inspired by storms, such as the 'Storm' interlude from the opera Peter Grimes by Benjamin Britten, 'Stormy Weather' sung by Etta James or 'Symphony No. 6, 4th Movement' by Beethoven.

What to do:

1. Ask the children to sit in a circle and explain that they are going to create a musical storm.

2. Sing a nursery rhyme to set the scene:
   I hear thunder, (x2)
   Hark don't you? (x2)
   Pitter patter raindrops, (x2)
   I'm wet through, so are you.

3. Start the rain with the children tapping two fingers against their open palms to create quiet, slow drops of rain.

4. Invite the children to make faster and louder sounds to show a storm arriving. They could rub their hands together for pouring rain, stamp their feet for thunder and clap loudly for lightning.

5. Try using groups of instruments for each part of the storm positioned around the circle. Use claves or wood blocks for the rain drops, maracas, shakers and rainsticks for the pouring rain, drums and cymbals for the thunder and triangles, guiros or glockenspiels for the lightning.

6. Walk around the circle and start the instrument groups in turn so the sound of the musical storm builds up. Try going backwards to make the storm die down again.

Be beside the seaside

Creating a soundscape in layers

What you need:

- Paintings, postcards or images of beaches
- Music about or inspired by the sea
- A selection of musical instruments
- DIY instruments (see 'Music workshop', page 42)
- Plastic bottles of water
- A recording device (e.g. a tablet)

Top tip

Try organising sounds to create other scenes too, such as the jungle, a moonlit night or a city street.

What's in it for the children?

Children will discover a different way to organise their musical sounds into sound pictures.

Taking it forward

- Add special features such as a flashing lighthouse, a foghorn, a shipwreck, some chattering dolphins, or a gang of pirates. Ask the children to think of different sounds to make for these events.
- Let the children take turns to conduct the different sounds and create their own soundscapes.

What to do:

1. Set the scene by talking about the seaside: the beach, sea, waves, swimming, boats, the weather and even pirates. Sing a song together such as 'I Do Like to Be Beside the Seaside' by John Glover-Kind, or play the children some classical music such as 'La Mer' ('The Sea') by Claude Debussy.

2. Look at paintings, postcards or images of beaches. Point out the foreground with the sandy beach, children playing, palm trees, etc. Point out the background with the sea and sky.

3. Sit the children in two rows and explain that they are going to create a soundscape or 'sound picture'.

4. The front row will be the foreground. Brainstorm some suitable sounds: sandpaper blocks and shakers (sand), claves (building sandcastles), tambourines (footsteps in sand) and children laughing and playing.

5. The back row will be the background. Brainstorm some suitable sounds: rainsticks, bottles of water, and guiros (splashing water, waves and boats); sliding along a glockenspiel (sunshine on water) and triangles (bird calls).

6. Practise each row and then put the sounds together to create the picture in layers. Record some seaside sound pictures and listen back. How could they be improved?

A trip on a train

Going on a journey using rhythms and sounds

What you need:

- A selection of musical instruments
- A recording device (e.g. a tablet)

Top tip

This works as a simple performance piece for a class assembly or concert.

What's in it for the children?

Children will be able to combine rhythm and sound ideas together to create a musical journey.

Taking it forward

- Add some rhythm instruments to accompany the train ostinato – claves, wood blocks, and tambourines.

- Record or film the trip on a train.

- Listen to the sounds of the city in George Gershwin's 'An American in Paris', or the sounds of the calm countryside in 'Fantasia on Greensleeves' by Vaughan Williams. Listen to some train journeys in 'Pacific 231' by Honegger and 'The Little Train of the Caipira' by Heitor Villa-Lobos.

- Adapt a nursery rhyme to fit the theme. For example, replace the lyrics to 'The Farmer's In His Den' with *The train goes fast and slow*, *'The train goes down the track'*, etc.

What to do:

1. To begin, practise some echo clapping and play the game 'Sticky loops' (see 'Ostinato loops', page 21).

2. Explain that the children are going to create a trip on a train using sounds. Talk about where they would like to go on the train.

3. Make a list of things they might see from the train window (such as a station, houses, a factory, farms, rivers and people waving).

4. Choose three different scenes and select some sounds using voices and instruments for each scene. For example, a station could have footsteps, a whistle and the sounds of a train engine. A farm could include animal sounds. A river could feature water sounds, ducks quacking and boats sailing.

5. Choose a rhythm to repeat for the train. Try saying 'trip on a train' over and over like an ostinato. Practise changing the speed or tempo to make the train go fast, then slowly and finally stop.

6. Put the ideas together. Ask some of the children to choose a partner and sit in rows as though on a train. Let them repeat the train ostinato ('trip on a train').

7. Choose some children to sit by the side of the train and make the sounds for the scenes (see Step 3) as the train goes past.

Just jamming

Spontaneous music-making

What you need:

- A music corner or table
- A selection of musical instruments and DIY instruments
- A selection of sound sources (materials that can be used to make sounds, e.g. pencils, newspaper, etc.)
- Examples of improvised music

Top tip

This is an important part of continuous provision but should be regularly refreshed with new musical sounds and stimuli.

What's in it for the children?

Children will be encouraged to enjoy spontaneous opportunities to make music, developing their creativity and cooperative skills.

Taking it forward

- Invite children who have worked together in the 'Just jamming' corner to show their music to the rest of the group. Some children may want to record their creations! See 'The Recording Studio', page 46.

- Adapt the musical provision to fit in with different topics. Can the children think of some changes to make in the 'Just jamming' corner to go with topics such as 'Ourselves' or 'Animals'?

What to do:

1. Set up a 'Just jamming' corner or table with easy access to a selection of musical instruments. Change the selection frequently. Explain that 'jamming' in music means making up music on the spot and playing it on your own or with friends.

2. Put out three or four different sound sources for the children to explore.

3. Encourage the children to visit the area as part of free play and explore and experiment with their voices, musical instruments and other sound sources.

4. Talk about improvisation and encourage the children to make up their own music on the spot. Remind them that their voices are musical instruments too.

5. Play children some improvised jazz music by artists such as Miles Davis or Herbie Hancock, or Indian classical music by Ravi Shankar.

6. Let them add their own DIY musical instruments to the selection and explore the sounds they can make (see 'Music workshop', page 42.

7. Ask the children to invite a friend or friends to come and play in the 'Just jamming' corner with them. Teach them a song to the lyrics of 'Wheels on the Bus':

   Come along and play with me,

   Play with me (x2)

   Come along and play with me,

   Just jamming together.

8. Take time to observe the children's spontaneous musical activities and join in as a musical partner when appropriate.

Duos, trios and quirky quartets

Making music in small groups

What you need:

- A selection of musical instruments and sound makers
- Whiteboards and pens
- Some pre-prepared graphic sound cards and notation cards (see 'Notation notes', page 49)
- Strips of card and felt-tip pens
- Four different-coloured hula hoops (optional)

Top tip

Some of these activities can happen informally in the 'Just jamming' corner, others can be more organised (see 'Taking it forward').

What to do:

1. Invite the children to find a partner and try some echo games (see 'Repeat after me', page 18).

2. Explain that when they play with a partner they are a duo playing a duet. Invite them to choose two instruments, either the same or different, and play together. Allow the children to swap instruments if they have picked two different ones. Can they copy each other exactly?

3. Give some graphic sound cards to the children to interpret in their duos, such as:

4. Can they write their own graphic sound cards to play?

5. Invite the children to form groups of three and explain that they are now a trio. Ask them to choose three different instruments or three of the same. Give them some more graphic sound cards with three different patterns.

6. Provide some notation cards for the children to play, using a different symbol for each instrument (see 'Notation notes', page 49).

What's in it for the children?

Children will play in different sizes of groups and learn the names for their ensembles, expanding their musical vocabulary. They will be able to notate music for each other to play.

Taking it forward

- Organise the children into quartets using four sorting hoops. Ask four children with four different instruments to each stand in their own hoop. Can they play all together and then one after the other?

- Provide the children with notation cards using four symbols to play in their quartets.

- Let the children write their own notation cards for the duos, trios and quartets to play.

- Play the children music by famous duos, trios and quartets such as Simon and Garfunkel, The Supremes and The Beatles.

Time to play together

Enjoying making music together

What you need:

- A selection of musical instruments, enough for each child
- Some well-known songs
- A recording device (e.g. a tablet)

What's in it for the children?

This activity builds on children's understanding of how to play lots of different instruments and follow a conductor. Children will hear the difference in sound texture when they all play together in small and large groups.

Taking it forward

- Let the children take turns to conduct the sounds using the timer or other signals (see the 'Conducting counts' section, pages 38 – 41).

- Play a game of 'Musical chains'. Place a selection of musical instruments in the middle of the circle. Invite a child to choose one instrument to play. The next child must repeat the sound and then add another of their own choice. How long can they make the musical chain?

What to do:

1. Ask the children to sit in a circle and place an instrument in front of each child. Use as many different instruments as you can find including untuned, tuned and DIY instruments.

2. Sort the instruments into groups if you prefer (see 'Be a sound sorter', page 47).

3. Show the children the 'Tick-tock timer': place both your arms bent in front of you like the hands on a clock at 12 o'clock. Move one hand round in a circle until it returns to the top.

4. Explain that the children can only play while the hands of the clock are moving.

5. Invite the children to pick up their instruments and follow the timer.

6. Try some different ways to play such as loudly or quietly, fast or slowly, high or low, solo or in a group, and so on.

7. Create a musical collage using solos, duets, trios, quartets and then everybody playing together. Talk about the texture of the music changing as more children play together.

8. Choose a song to learn together and play instruments when directed. For example, *'If you're happy and you know it, make some sound*s'.

Making music for Anansi

Exploring the sounds of West Africa

What you need:

- A version of one of the Anansi stories, such as *The Leopard's Drum* by Jessica Souhami, or others available online
- A world map and recordings of West African music
- Lots of different-sized drums, including DIY ones
- Animal masks or materials to make some
- Cardboard, scissors, strong cardboard box with a lid, bobby pins and sticky tape (optional)

What to do:

1. Tell the children they will be listening to a traditional West African folktale, pointing to West Africa on a map. Explain that they will be making music to accompany and embellish the story. Discover some West African music on YouTube or at www.mamalisa.com.

2. Share your chosen Anansi story with the children, introducing the different characters such as Anansi the spider, Osebo the leopard, Nyame the sky god and Mmoatia the fairy.

3. Sit in a drumming circle (see 'Drumming drives', page 32) and provide each child with a drum. Try drumming together to some recorded West African music.

4. Make up drumming patterns for the different animals making rhythms using the syllables of their names. Play around with volume and tempo, using short and long sounds.

5. Notate the names using dots (.) and dashes (_), (see 'Repeat after me', page 18).

6. Try out different voices for the animals. Osebo the leopard could have a very low voice. What sort of voice could Anansi have?

7. Retell the story and let children act out the parts of the characters.

What's in it for the children?

Children will find out about an African folktale, act out a traditional story and make music together.

Taking it forward

- Make masks for the different animals in the story.
- Make a Kalimba (a type of thumb piano) using a strong cardboard box. Cut a round hand-sized hole in the top and tape four or five open bobby pins halfway across the hole. Decorate the box in bright colours. The children should use their thumbs to pluck the pins to make sounds.

The musical donkey

Exploring the sounds of India

What you need:

- A version of 'The Musical Donkey', an Indian story from the Panchatantra (an ancient Indian collection of animal stories), available online

- Indian classical music

- Pictures of Indian instruments, including tanpuras, sitars and tabla

- A recording of a tanpura, available online

- A selection of tuned percussion instruments such as chime bars and xylophones (see 'Useful resources', page 5)

What to do:

1. Share the story of 'The Musical Donkey'.

2. Invite the children to act out the story. Can they recreate some donkey singing sounds? Use Indian classical music to accompany the story.

3. Look at pictures of Indian instruments and discuss them. How might they be played? What might they sound like?

4. Explain that the tanpura instrument produces a drone sound – a long sustained note. Play the children a recording of a tanpura and listen to the drone.

5. Explain to the children that in Indian music, a raga is a scale or sequence of notes. The Bhupali raga is a pentatonic scale known as the 'evening' raga.

6. Set up the Bhupali raga on a xylophone or tuned percussion instrument using the notes C, D, E, G and A (see 'Pentatonic patterns' page 34).

7. Let the children take turns to improvise or make up their own patterns using the raga over the top of the tanpura drone recording.

What's in it for the children?

Children will discover an Indian moral story and explore Indian music and instruments.

Taking it forward

- Talk about the moral of 'The Musical Donkey' (taking care to listen to friends).

- Listen to the sound of the donkey in 'Characters with Long Ears' from the 'The Carnival of the Animals' by Camille Saint-Saëns. Can the children hear the donkey braying?

- Play children examples of different instruments using this interactive sound guide: www.aaastateofplay.com/the-wide-world-of-music-a-guide-to-100-musical-instruments-interactive

Top tip ⭐

Compare and contrast different versions of the story online.

Shadow puppets
Making musical stories with puppets

What you need:

- Examples of Chinese shadow puppet theatre
- A recording of the Chinese folksong 'Mo Li Hua', available online
- Examples of Chinese music played on Chinese instruments such as the erhu, guzheng, dizi (or bamboo flute) and yangqin
- Pictures of Chinese instruments
- A selection of metal instruments such as bells, triangles and cymbals
- A selection of tuned musical instruments (see 'Useful resources', page 5)
- Black sugar paper, templates, scissors and sticks

What to do:

1. Show the children some examples of Chinese shadow puppet theatre. Can they figure out how it works?

2. Introduce the children to a Chinese folksong, 'Mo Li Hua' ('Jasmine Flower'). What do they think of the song?

3. Listen to some music played on Chinese instruments (see 'What you need' section). Look at pictures of the instruments and talk about them.

4. Let the children experiment with some metal instruments to make some ringing, dinging and chiming sounds. Encourage them to make a sound and then leave a space for it to ring so they can listen until it fades away.

5. Add a metal tuned instrument using the pentatonic scale (C D E G A) and let the children play up and down the scale at different tempos.

6. Combine layers of the tuned instrument sounds and the metal sounds to create a unique piece inspired by Chinese music.

What's in it for the children?

Children will be able to make some Chinese-inspired music and create shadow puppets to tell a story.

Taking it forward

- Try making some shadows using hand shapes in front of a light source. Can the children make flapping butterflies, running rabbits or snapping alligators?

- Make some shadow puppets by cutting out templates from black sugar paper. Try making people and animals. Mount them on sticks and let the children use them to tell a story to go with the Chinese-inspired music.

- Discover more music from different continents at www.putumayo.com.

Sounds of steel pans

Learning about the Caribbean

What you need:

- A steel pan or access to a steel pan app
- Different-sized saucepan lids
- Xylophone beaters
- Shakers and guiros
- Cardboard tins with metal bottoms (e.g. coffee or milk powder tins or crisp tubes)
- Small bouncy rubber balls

What to do:

1. Listen to some steel pan music from the Caribbean, available online and as playlists on streaming websites.
2. If possible, let the children have a go on a real steel pan and listen to the sounds it makes. Alternatively, download a steel pan app and let them take turns to make sounds.
3. Improvise your own steel pan sounds by using different-sized saucepan lids and xylophone beaters. Listen to the sounds and try to arrange them in order of pitch: low, middle and high.
4. Play along to some steel pan music using body percussion together with shakers and guiros.

Top tip

Accompany the activity with a book set in the Caribbean such as *Drum Dream Girl* by Margarita Engle and illustrated by Rafael López, *Tales from the Caribbean* by Trish Cooke or *Caribbean Dream* by Rachel Isadora.

What's in it for the children?

Children will discover steel pan music and enjoy making their own instruments.

Taking it forward

- Make a bouncy tube drum. Use empty crisp tubes or tins with metal bottoms and plastic lids. Cover them in paper and decorate the outside. Put a small bouncy rubber ball inside and replace the lid. Shake the tin and listen to the DIY steel pan sounds!
- Listen to some other genres from the Caribbean such as reggae music or calypso music. Listen to Caribbean songs such as 'Tingalayo' or 'Four White Horses'.